■SCHOLAST

READ & RESP⌀ND

Bringing the best books to life in the classroom

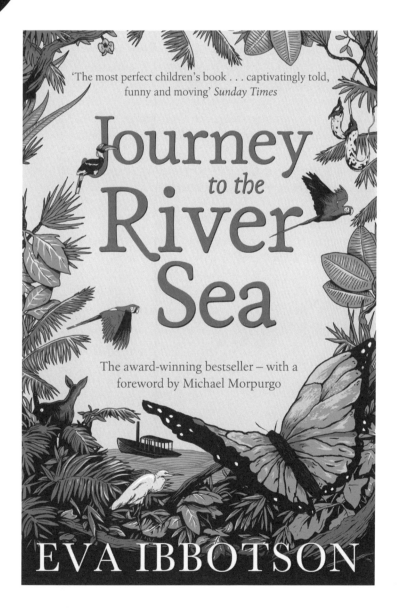

'The most perfect children's book . . . captivatingly told, funny and moving' *Sunday Times*

Journey to the River Sea

The award-winning bestseller – with a foreword by Michael Morpurgo

EVA IBBOTSON

FOR AGES 7–11

Scholastic Education, an imprint of Scholastic Ltd
Book End, Range Road, Witney, Oxfordshire, OX29 0YD
Registered office: Westfield Road, Southam, Warwickshire CV47 0RA

Printed and bound by Ashford Colour Press
© 2018 Scholastic Ltd
1 2 3 4 5 6 7 8 9 8 9 0 1 2 3 4 5 6 7

British Library Cataloguing-in-Publication Data
A catalogue record for this book is available from the British Library.
ISBN 978-1407-17506-5

Author Jillian Powell
Editorial team Audrey Stokes, Vicki Yates, Suzanne Adams, Julia Roberts
Series designer Neil Salt and Alice Duggan
Designer Alice Duggan
Illustrator Stu McLellan / Beehive Illustration

Acknowledgements

Photographs
Page 8: Eva Ibbotson, Curtis Brown Group Ltd.

Every effort has been made to trace copyright holders for the works reproduced in this book, and the publishers apologise for any inadvertent omissions.

CONTENTS ▼

How to use Read & Respond in your classroom...

Read & Respond provides teaching ideas related to a specific well-loved children's book. Each Read & Respond book is divided into the following sections:

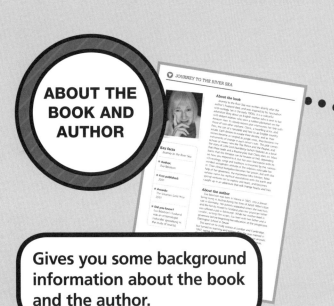

ABOUT THE BOOK AND AUTHOR

Gives you some background information about the book and the author.

GUIDED READING

Breaks the book down into sections and gives notes for using it with guided reading groups. A bookmark has been provided on page 12 containing comprehension questions. The children can be directed to refer to these as they read.

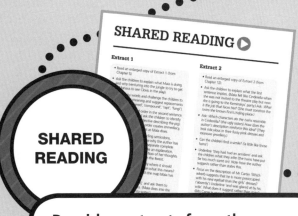

SHARED READING

Provides extracts from the children's book with associated notes for focused work. There is also one non-fiction extract that relates to the children's book.

GRAMMAR, PUNCTUATION & SPELLING

Provides word-level work related to the children's book so you can teach grammar, punctuation and spelling in context.

PLOT, CHARACTER & SETTING

Contains activity ideas focused on the plot, characters and the setting of the story.

PLOT, CHARACTER & SETTING ▶

1. Storyboard

Objective
To identify main ideas drawn from more than one paragraph and to summarise these

What you need
Copies of Journey to the River Sea; drawing materials

Cross-curricular link
Art and design

What to do
...

2. The amazing Amazon

Objective
To distinguish between statements of fact and opinion

What you need
Copies of Journey to the River Sea, photocopiable page 29 'The amazing Amazon'

Cross-curricular link
Geography

What to do
...

READ&RESPOND Journey to the River Sea 25

GET WRITING

Provides writing activities related to the children's book. These activities may be based directly on the children's book or be broadly based on the themes and concepts of the story.

TALK ABOUT IT

Has speaking and listening activities related to the children's book. These activities may be based directly on the children's book or be broadly based on the themes and concepts of the story.

ASSESSMENT

Contains short activities that will help you assess whether the children have understood concepts and curriculum objectives. They are designed to be informal activities to feed into your planning.

❝ The titles are great fun to use and cover exactly the range of books that children most want to read. It makes it easy to explore texts fully and ensure the children want to keep on reading more. ❞

Chris Flanagan, Year 5 Teacher, St Thomas of Canterbury Primary School

Activities

The activities follow the same format:

- **Objective:** the objective for the lesson. It will be based upon a curriculum objective, but will often be more specific to the focus being covered.

- **What you need:** a list of resources you need to teach the lesson, including printable pages.

- **What to do:** the activity notes.

- **Differentiation:** this is provided where specific and useful differentiation advice can be given to support and/or extend the learning in the activity. Differentiation by providing additional adult support has not been included as this will be at a teacher's discretion based upon specific children's needs and ability, as well as the availability of support.

The activities are numbered for reference within each section and should move through the text sequentially – so you can use the lesson while you are reading the book. Once you have read the book, most of the activities can be used in any order you wish.

CURRICULUM LINKS

Section	Activity	Curriculum objectives
Guided reading		Comprehension: To ask questions to improve their understanding. Spoken language: To use spoken language to develop understanding.
Shared reading	1	Comprehension: To discuss their understanding and explore the meaning of words in context.
	2	Comprehension: To draw inferences...justifying them with evidence.
	3	Comprehension: To discuss their understanding and explore the meaning of words in context.
	4	Comprehension: To identify how language...contributes to meaning.
Grammar, punctuation & spelling	1	Vocabulary, grammar and punctuation: To find how words are related by meaning as synonyms and antonyms.
	2	Vocabulary, grammar and punctuation: To use semicolons...to mark boundaries between independent clauses; to use a colon to introduce a list; to punctuate bullet points consistently.
	3	Vocabulary, grammar and punctuation: To use modal verbs to indicate degrees of possibility.
	4	Vocabulary, grammar and punctuation: To use relative clauses beginning with who, which, where; to use commas to clarify meaning.
	5	Vocabulary, grammar and punctuation: To use passive verbs to affect the presentation of information in a sentence.
	6	Transcription: To distinguish between homophones and other words that are often confused.
Plot, character & setting	1	Comprehension: To identify main ideas drawn from more than one paragraph and to summarise these.
	2	Comprehension: To distinguish between statements of fact and opinion.
	3	Spoken language: To ask relevant questions to extend their understanding and knowledge.
	4	Spoken language: To give well-structured descriptions, explanations and narratives.
	5	Comprehension: To draw inferences such as inferring characters' feelings, thoughts and motives from their actions.
	6	Comprehension: To predict what might happen from details stated and implied.
	7	Spoken language: To give well-structured descriptions...for different purposes. Comprehension: To draw inferences such as inferring characters'...thoughts.
	8	Spoken language: To give well-structured...explanations.

Section	Activity	Curriculum objectives
Talk about it	1	Spoken language: To participate in...role play, improvisations and debates.
	2	Spoken language: To maintain attention and participate actively in collaborative conversations, staying on topic.
	3	Spoken language: To use spoken language to develop understanding; to participate in discussions.
	4	Spoken language: To give well-structured...explanations...for different purposes.
	5	Comprehension: To distinguish between statements of fact and opinion.
	6	Spoken language: To use spoken language to develop understanding through speculating, hypothesising, imagining and exploring ideas.
Get writing	1	Composition: To identify the audience for and purpose of the writing, selecting the appropriate form.
	2	Composition: To note and develop initial ideas, drawing on reading where necessary.
	3	Composition: To identify the audience for and purpose of the writing, selecting the appropriate form and using other similar writing as models for their own.
	4	Composition: To identify the audience for and purpose of the writing, selecting the appropriate form.
	5	Comprehension: To discuss and evaluate how authors use language, including figurative language, considering the impact on the reader.
	6	Comprehension: To draw inferences, such as inferring characters' feelings, thoughts and motives from their actions.
Assessment	1	Comprehension: To summarise the main ideas drawn from more than one paragraph.
	2	Comprehension: To identify and discuss themes.
	3	Comprehension: To summarise the main ideas drawn from more than one paragraph.
	4	Comprehension: To explain and discuss their understanding of what they have read; to provide reasoned justifications for their views.
	5	Comprehension: To explain and discuss their understanding of what they have read; to provide reasoned justifications for their views.
	6	Comprehension: To ask questions to improve their understanding. Spoken language: To use spoken language to develop understanding.

Key facts
Journey to the River Sea

◉ **Author:**
Eva Ibbotson

◉ **First published:**
2001

◉ **Awards:**
The Smarties Gold Prize
2001

◉ **Did you know?**
Eva Ibbotson's husband
was an entomologist
(naturalist specialising in
the study of insects)

About the book

Journey to the River Sea was written shortly after the author's husband died, and was inspired by his fascination with ecology. Set in the early 1900s, it is a colourful adventure story about an English orphan who is sent to live with distant relatives who own a rubber plantation on the Amazon river. Its closely-woven plot intertwines her fate with those of two other orphans: Clovis, a travelling actor, and Finn, the son of a naturalist and heir to an English country estate. Each desires to escape their destiny, and as their stories become as tangled as jungle vines, they become the instruments of change in each other's lives. The plot carries echoes of classic tales like *The Prince and the Pauper*, and the story of *Little Lord Fauntleroy* (which features as a book that Maia reads and a theatre play that Clovis stars in). Maia learns that the Amazon can be heaven or hell, depending on how you respond to it, but her own fascination with its rich ecology, songs and traditions is thwarted by the narrow-minded xenophobic attitude of the relatives who take her in. Their clinical bungalow becomes her prison, but with the help of her governess, the mysterious Miss Minton, Maia (whose name has mythical associations with the earth and spring) ventures out to explore and learn, and becomes caught up in an adventure that will change hearts and lives.

About the author

Eva Ibbotson was born in Vienna in 1925, into a Jewish family living in Austria during the time of Adolf Hitler's Nazi rule in Germany. Her parents separated when she was two, and the family moved to Scotland after her physician father was offered a job in Edinburgh. While her mother lived in London, writing film scripts, Eva lived with her father and a governess before beginning her education at the progressive Dartington School in Devon.

She went on to study science at London and Cambridge, but turned to teaching and writing after she was married in 1947, saying she preferred not to do experiments on animals. She began writing magazine stories and television dramas, publishing her first book for children, *The Great Ghost Rescue*, in 1975.

After the death of her husband, she sought solace by writing more serious, historical novels. The first of these was *Journey to the River Sea*. Her children's books have been shortlisted for awards, including the Carnegie Medal and the Roald Dahl Funny Prize. She died at the age of 85 in October 2011, a few months before her last story, *One Dog and his Boy*, was published.

GUIDED READING ▶

Cover and Chapters 1 to 3

Look together at the cover of *Journey to the River Sea*. Ask the children what sort of story they think this will be. Next read the back cover blurb. What makes us want to read the story? Invite ideas from the class. Read the author's introduction. Ask the children to explain what sparked the idea for the book (hearing about the city of Manaus in the Amazon). Bring out the contrast that the author sets up between the wealthy rubber plantation owners and the city they build, and the jungle that is wild, untamed and irrepressible. Ask: *What tells us that the jungle, over time, reclaimed the city?* (Today the grass grows through the roof and monkeys clamber over it.)

Read Chapter 1. Ask the children to summarise Maia's situation. (Her parents have died in a train crash and she is an orphan. She is at school in England but is being sent to live with distant relatives in Brazil.) Ask: *Who will go with her?* (a governess, Miss Minton) Explain that in 1910, when the story is set, it was common for children in families who could afford it, to be schooled at home by a governess. Ask the children how they would feel about the prospect (excited, anxious). Refer to the refrain Maia reads in an old book about the Amazon being 'a hell or a heaven'. How are these represented in her reaction and those of her classmates? (She sees it as a rich new world to explore; they think only of bugs and alligators and dangerous Indians.)

Read Chapter 2, as far as the chapter break. Focus on Clovis. Ask: *How is he similar to or different from Maia?* (They are both orphans, but unlike Maia, Clovis does not relish adventure and is homesick all the time.) Contin *ointments for Maia?* (The twins are spiteful and nasty; the schooling is dull; she is not able to explore outside.) *Why have the Carters taken Maia in?* (because they need the money) At the end of the chapter, review the glimmers of hope that exist for Maia: her interest in the Indian servants and their community, and Miss Minton's ruse to enable her to have more interesting lessons.

Chapters 4 to 8

Read on through Chapter 4. Pause to note significant new characters (Sergei and Olga, Professor Glastonberry, the two private detectives nicknamed 'the crows') and a key plot development: the search for a mysterious boy who must be found and returned to England. Ask: *Why is Maia upset to miss the theatre play?* (She has promised Clovis she will be there.) At the end of the chapter, ask the children what they think she might do, and how she might try to get there. (Get to the theatre, by navigating her way along the water channels she has seen on the map that lead to the city.)

Read Chapter 5, pausing after the opening sentence to raise question 9 on the Guided Reading bookmark. Reflect on the situation which gives Maia her opportunity. (Miss Minton has to retire with a migraine.) Ask: *Do you think Maia is brave or foolhardy to attempt the trip? Do you think the Indian boy may become another important character and, if so, why?* As they read the description of the jungle, encourage them to note questions 8 and 10 on the bookmark, and revisit them as they read on.

Read Chapter 6 as far as the chapter break. What more have we learned about the mysterious 'wanted' boy? (His name is Finn; he is in hiding; the police chief, Professor Glastonberry and the Indian servants are conspiring to prevent him being sent back to England.) Remind them that the children, including Maia, already feel that they want to protect the boy too. Encourage them to speculate on what 'Westwood' may be: A school? A prison? A house? Raise question 5 on the bookmark, and encourage children to look out for and consider other examples as they read on. Read the rest of the chapter. Ask: *What has happened that Clovis was dreading?* (His voice is beginning to break when he is playing a young boy's part.) *Can you suggest how Clovis might play a part in the developing plot?* (There is a boy who does not want to return to England, while Clovis does.) Consider question 2 on the bookmark.

Read through Chapter 7. Pause at the end to review the threads that are coming together: Maia has made friends with the Indian servants and through them has found the 'Indian boy' who rescued her, who is Finn, the son of Bernard Taverner. What plan is he now hatching? (to get Clovis back to England in his place) Consider question 1 on the bookmark.

Read on through Chapter 8, as far as the first chapter break. Ask: *How are the 'crows' being thwarted?* (The Indians and Colonel da Silva are collaborating to hide Taverner's son.) *How does the boy's fate become of interest to the Carters?* (There is a large reward for finding him.) Continue reading as far as 'And now the boy had vanished'. *Why does Maia feel anxious when they decide to search the hut?* (She thinks Clovis is hiding in there.) *What has happened to him?* (Miss Minton had hidden him there, but he has since vanished.) Read to the end of the chapter. Ask: *Why does Finn's idea suit both boys?* (Finn wants to stay; Clovis yearns to go home to England.) Raise question 6 on the bookmark and again encourage children to look out for further examples in later chapters.

Chapters 9 to 13

Read Chapter 9 and briefly review what we learn about Westwood and the reason for the crows' search. Ask question 4 on the bookmark. (Finn's grandfather wants him to come home to inherit the family estate as his uncle Dudley has been killed in a hunting accident and he is the only male heir.) Read the next chapter and encourage the children to extract key plot developments. (Maia has taken the keys to the museum so that Clovis can hide in the cellar and be discovered there by the crows who will assume he is Taverner's son.) Ask: *What is Finn teaching Clovis and why?* (all about Westwood so he can convince Sir Aubrey he is his grandson) Highlight what we learn about Miss Minton (she seems to be complicit with the children's plans, and also there is a suggestion that she knew Bernard Taverner).

Read on through Chapter 11. Ask the children how Carter upset and angered the Indians. (He broke his promise and destroyed the longhouse which they believed the medicine man's spirit inhabited.) Ask: *What must Clovis now teach Maia, to help them to carry out their plan?* (How to act in order to convince the twins that she has given Finn away unintentionally.) Ask: *Why is the plan urgent?* (The ship sails in three days and the crows are now so sick of the Amazon they just want to go home.)

Read Chapter 12. Ask: *Does everything go to plan?* (No: Sergei interrupts before Maia can reveal the exact hiding place to the twins.) Continue reading through Chapter 13. Ask: *Why is Maia afraid that Miss Minton will give them away?* (She will recognise Finn and Clovis.) *What happens instead?* (She convinces the crows that Clovis *is* Finn Taverner, so they lose interest in Finn, thinking he is an Indian servant.)

Chapters 14 to 18

Read Chapter 14 as far as the first break. Ask question 3 on the bookmark (Miss Minton was the housemaid at Westwood who helped Bernard escape, and she has known all along about their plan to save Finn from going back.) Consider question 7 on the bookmark. Continue reading to the end of the chapter, noting shifts in the narrative (to Colonel da Silva, Professor Glastonberry, the Carters, the Keminskys). Ask: *What does Maia want to do?* (Go with Finn on the *Arabella* to the Xanti.) *How do you think Miss Minton is feeling at this point?* (She feels she must continue in her duties, but she is tempted by the idea of adventure and becoming a naturalist like Bernard.) Discuss questions 11 and 12 on the bookmark. Read Chapter 15, pausing at the end to highlight the irony: Sir Aubrey seeing a likeness between Clovis and a family ancestor.

Read Chapter 16 and review how key characters are feeling: Maia and Miss Minton becoming more unsettled, Finn unexpectedly lonely, Mr Carter worrying about his finances, the twins preoccupied with their reward money. Read Chapter 17, pausing at the end to encourage the children to speculate on what has happened. (Has Sir Aubrey died?) Continue to the end of Chapter 18. Review the circumstances that leave Maia in danger. (Miss Minton and the Indian servants being away, the twins causing a fire, Carter only concerned with his eyeball collection.)

Chapter 19 to the end

Read Chapter 19. Ask: *How are we left in suspense?* (We don't know if Maia has survived.) Review question 6 on the bookmark. Read Chapter 20, as far as the first chapter break. Ask: *Do you remember the first time Finn rescued Maia?* (When she was lost trying to get to Manaus.) Continue to the end of Chapter 21. Ask: *Why was Miss Minton feeling torn?* (She knows she should take Maia home, but she also feels the lure of adventure.) Read the next two chapters. Ask: *Do you feel the good and bad characters have got what they deserve?* (The twins now have to work like servants for the mean and snobbish Lady Parsons, while Maia, Finn, Miss Minton and the Professor are enjoying the freedom and fun of living among the friendly Xanti Indians.) *What brings their idyll to an end?* (The discovery of Miss Minton's corset triggers a search party.) Consider question 13 on the bookmark.

Read to the end of the book. Ask: *How is it a happy ending?* Reflect on the fates of the key characters, and how they have been changed during the story. Raise question 14 on the bookmark.

Journey to the River Sea
by Eva Ibbotson

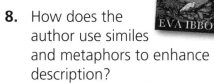

Focus on...
Meaning

1. Maia, Finn and Clovis are all orphans. How does this affect their lives and drive the plot line?

2. Can you suggest any parallels in the story with the tale of *Little Lord Fauntleroy*?

3. Explain the connection between Miss Minton and Bernard Taverner.

4. How does Dudley Taverner's accidental death affect events in the plot?

Focus on...
Organisation

5. How does the author use chapter breaks or pauses to shift the time or focus of the story line?

6. How does the author create suspense at chapter ends to make us want to read on?

7. Who or what links past and present times and generations in the story?

Journey to the River Sea
by Eva Ibbotson

Focus on...
Language and features

8. How does the author use similes and metaphors to enhance description?

9. Maia sometimes feels like Cinderella; which characters remind us of the ugly sisters and why?

10. Note any proper names of plants, animals or places belonging to the Amazon.

Focus on...
Purpose, viewpoints and effects

11. Name some characters who view the Amazon as heaven and some who view it as hell.

12. How do you think the author views the Amazon (heaven or hell)? Explain why.

13. What moral or message do you think the story conveys about being a traveller?

14. Would the book encourage you to want to visit the Amazon or not? Explain why.

SHARED READING ▶

Extract 1

- Read an enlarged copy of Extract 1 (from Chapter 5).

- Ask the children to explain what Maia is doing and why (venturing into the jungle to try to get to Manaus to see Clovis in the play).

- Circle tricky words and challenge the children to explain their meaning and suggest replacements ('rootling', 'tethered', 'compound', 'rapt', 'fungi').

- Focus on the word order in the second sentence. Circle 'tethered', and ask the children to identify the part of speech (adjective describing the pig). Suggest that the word order creates immediacy, because we notice things as Maia does.

- Focus on punctuation, circling semicolons, colons and ellipses. Analyse why the author has used them: semicolons to separate complete clauses, a colon to anticipate an explanation, and ellipses to suggest the flow of her thoughts and her movement through the forest.

- Underline the words 'exactly where it should have been'. Can they explain what this means? (The path corresponds with the map Maia has studied.)

- Circle the word 'plunged,' and ask them to explain what it suggests. (Maia dives into the jungle as you might into water.)

- Can they find a simile? ('glowed like a jewel')

- Ask: *Why do you think Maia says the words aloud?* (She is alone, and she is so overcome.) *Why do you think she would not object to the 'rotten' smell?* (Because it is natural decay, leaves and fungi.)

- Underline 'but the sun could not be relied upon'. Can the children explain what this means? (She cannot always see it, because at times the dense foliage obscures it.)

Extract 2

- Read an enlarged copy of Extract 2 (from Chapter 12).

- Ask the children to explain what the first sentence implies. (Maia felt like Cinderella when she was not invited to the theatre play but now she is going to the Keminskys' party.) Ask: *What is the job that faces her?* (She must convince the twins she knows Finn's hiding place.)

- Ask: *Which characters do the twins resemble in* Cinderella? (the ugly sisters) *How does the author's description reinforce this idea?* (They look ridiculous in their fussy pink dresses and excessive jewellery.)

- Can the children find a simile? ('a little like those hams')

- Underline 'they had had an accident' and ask the children what they infer (the twins have put far too much scent on). Note how the author suggests rather than states this.

- Focus on the description of Mr Carter. Which adverb suggests that he is more preoccupied with his new eyeball than the girls' dresses? ('absently') Underline 'and was glared at by his wife'. What does it suggest rather than state? (Mrs Carter is angry because she resents Maia looking more attractive than her daughters.)

- Ask: *How are the twins feeling?* (jealous of Maia) *What suggests this?* (their nasty comments to her, and they do not look pleased when they see her) *What does the accident with the scent tell us?* (that they were bickering)

- Ask: *What do you think Minty thinks?* (She knows that Maia looks much nicer than the twins do, and will not let them spoil it.)

Extract 3

- Read an enlarged copy of Extract 3 (from Chapter 13).

- Ask the children why they think Maia's voice is quiet. (She is worried because she is afraid Miss Minton will give them away when she recognises Clovis.)

- Ask: *Why are Miss Minton and Maia so upset when the sloth is smashed?* (They know how much effort and time Professor Glastonberry has spent on it.)

- Challenge the children to identify incomplete sentences. ('The skeleton', 'In the lab', 'Still no chance to warn her governess') Can they complete them? What effect do these incomplete sentences have? (They convey Maia's reluctance to talk, and help create pace.)

- Ask: *Why is Maia so horrified when the boy emerges?* (She expects to see Clovis but it is Finn.)

- Focus on the description of the boy. Circle the adjectives and present participles: 'furious', 'thrashing', 'shouting', 'jabbering', 'cursing', 'screaming'. Invite the children to suggest other adjectives to describe him ('wild', 'untamed', 'savage', 'angry').

- Circle the word 'dialect' and ask if they know what it means (a local language). Which other word refers to his language? ('babble')

- Ask what effect the three questions at the end of the text create (suspense because we want to read on to find out what has happened and why the plan has gone awry).

- Ask: *What will be Maia's fear now?* (that Miss Minton will give Finn away) *What, in fact, does Miss Minton do and why?* (She asks Finn to come out, knowing that it will be Clovis, because she understands the plan and wants to help them. NB. Children will need to read beyond the end of the extract to find this out.)

Extract 4

- Read an enlarged copy of Extract 4, the non-fiction extract.

- Ask the children where they think the text might appear and who it is aimed at (on a website or in a brochure by a travel company, for people interested in exploring the Amazon).

- Highlight tricky or unfamiliar words or phrases, challenging children to explain their meaning and suggest replacements. ('foray', 'wilderness', 'tributaries', 'flora and fauna', 'trill', 'eco-systems')

- Ask: *What is the advantage of travelling by kayak as opposed to a river cruise boat? What kind of people might this holiday appeal to?* (adventurous travellers)

- Identify the tone (persuasive) and ask children to find examples of persuasive language. ('Do you dream?', 'a dazzling array…awaits you')

- Circle the verb 'snake'. Why is this a good verb to use when talking about the Amazon? What image does it help to convey?

- Revise alliteration, underlining or circling examples ('foray/forest'; 'delve/deeper'; 'flora and fauna'; 'towering trees')

- Circle the word 'teem' and challenge the children to explain its meaning and identify its homophone ('teem' = abound; 'team' = group of people working together).

- Focus on the precautions advised at the end of the piece. Ask: *Which characters in the book do you think would love to explore by canoe or kayak* (Finn and Maia) *and which would see it as dangerous and nasty?* (The Carters)

- Encourage the children to give subjective opinions on whether they would be persuaded to go on a trip like this, or not, and to give reasons to back up their answers.

Extract 1

She had looked at the Indian huts so often from her window that it was strange to be walking past them. The little rootling pig was there, tethered, and a few chickens, but the Indians were all away, working in the forest or the house.

The beginning of the path was exactly where it should have been, with a narrow plank over the stream it followed. Maia plunged into the forest.

Away from the compound, the great trees grew more thickly; dappled creepers wound round the trunks searching for the light; a scarlet orchid, hanging from a branch, glowed like a jewel in a shaft of sun.

'Oh, but it is beautiful!' she said aloud, and drew the damp, earthy, slightly rotten smell into her lungs.

But it was a mistake to be so rapt about the beauty of nature because the path was not quite as simple as it had appeared on the map. She knew she had to keep the sun on her right; but the sun could not be relied upon: sometimes the canopy of leaves was so dense that she seemed to be walking in twilight. And the streams kept branching… She stayed beside the widest of them, but the path made by the rubber-gatherers was overgrown; she stumbled over roots of trees, trod on strange fungi, orange and mauve…Sometimes a smaller stream cut across her path and she had to jump it or paddle. Once something ran through the trees ahead of her, a grey snuffling creature…

She couldn't have told the exact moment at which she knew she was lost.

Extract 2

This time Maia did not feel like Cinderella. She was going to the party as well as the twins, and as she dressed she almost forgot the job that faced her when she reached Sergei's house. Her dress was new, the last one the matron of the school in London had bought with her before she went away, and it was very pretty. A dark blue, rustling silk cut like an Elizabethan dress, with a very full skirt and a row of tiny pearl buttons on the bodice. Minty had brushed out her waist-length hair and left it loose, and the twins, when they saw her, did not look pleased.

'You're too skinny to wear a low neckline.'

'And your hair will get into a mess.'

'Shall I plait it again?' Maia asked Miss Minton, and her governess pursed up her mouth and said, 'No.'

The twins were dressed in their favourite party pink; rather a *fleshy* pink, which was perhaps a pity because their short necks coming out of a double row of ruffles made them look a little like those hams one sees on butchers' slabs near Christmas. They wore several bracelets, so that they tinkled as they walked, and they had had an accident with their mother's scent. Beatrice had taken some and sprinkled it behind her ears and then Gwendolyn had tried to take it from her and the stopper had come off, so that both of them smelled violently of 'Passion in the Night'.

Mrs Carter did not mean to stay behind in the bungalow. She had invited herself to play bridge in the club in Manaus. Mr Carter came out to say goodbye, holding a small box containing the eye of a murderer who had been hanged in Pentonville prison. It had arrived that morning and excited him very much.

'Very nice,' he said absently, looking at Maia's dress, and was glared at by his wife. 'The twins too…very fetching,' – and he hurried back into his study.

Extract 3

'He's in the cellar.' Maia's voice was very quiet. She turned her head away.

'Where's that? How do you get down there?'

'There's a trapdoor. It's under the giant sloth. The skeleton. In the lab.'

The crows barged ahead, holding Maia by the arm, and Miss Minton followed. Still no chance to warn her governess.

They reached the sloth. 'There, look. You can see the handle,' said Mr Low.

Mr Trapwood pushed him aside and caught the edge of the stand with his arm.

The sloth crashed to the ground.

Miss Minton and Maia cried out, seeing the jumbled bones.

'There it is! Come on. Heave!'

Mr Trapwood heaved. The door creaked slowly upwards…And out of the dark hole there sprang, not a cowering, frightened boy, but a furious, thrashing figure. A boy with black hair and a headband who charged at the two men, shouting and jabbering in an Indian dialect. The crows tried to grab his arm – and missed. The Indian boy ran past Mr Low, but was tripped up by Mr Trapwood and stumbled, cursing in his strange babble; screaming like a trapped animal.

Maia gave a moan of despair and stood there, her hand over her mouth. What was Finn doing here? What had gone so terribly wrong? And where was Clovis?

Extract 4

Amazon Adventures
Do you dream of being a jungle explorer?

One of the best ways to foray into the Amazon forest is by boat: it is often said that rivers are the roadways of the Amazon. If it is a day trip you are after, you can take one of the motorized cruise boats from Manaus. But to delve deeper into the wilderness and explore the many channels and creeks that snake through the jungle, the best way to travel is by kayak.

The towering trees and meandering tributaries teem with life and a dazzling array of flora and fauna awaits you. The only sounds you hear will be the plop of your paddle, the rustling of troops of howler monkeys in the tree canopy or the trill song of tropical birds. Gliding silently along these backwaters gives you the best chance to see wildlife that travellers on motorised riverboats may miss.

Remember to pack your camera and binoculars as you may spot three-toed sloths, caiman or colourful macaws, piranha fish or pink river dolphins.

Our kayak trips run during the rainy season from November to June, when the river rises to flood low-lying forests along its banks, making many smaller channels passable. This allows you to paddle along small tributaries of the flooded forest, visiting remote villages and exploring fragile eco-systems. There may be the chance to hear from the 'ribeirinhos' or homesteaders who live on the banks of the river about how they fish, hunt and collect rubber. As there can be occasional storms, you need to prepare for wet weather, wind and high waves. Wear cover-up clothing to protect against biting insects including mosquitoes, as malaria is a risk along with dengue fever, burrowing bugs and traveller's diarrhoea. Taking precautions against these will help you enjoy your Amazonian adventure and make lifelong memories.

GRAMMAR, PUNCTUATION & SPELLING ▶

1. Word search

> **Objective**
> To find and use synonyms and antonyms.
>
> **What you need**
> Copies of *Journey to the River Sea*.

What to do

- To begin the lesson, read together the paragraph describing Mr Carter's study (Chapter 4) from 'The room was dismal' to 'cabinets'. Ask the children to identify adjectives and list them on the board ('dismal', 'dark', 'dusty', 'untidy'). Use one adjective to revise the meaning of synonyms, for example 'dismal' ('drab', 'dingy', 'gloomy', 'dreary'). Ask the children to suggest synonyms for each of the other words and write the best suggestions on the board.

- Arrange the children in pairs and challenge them to draft one or two sentences using synonyms to extend the description. Suggest they could describe Mr Carter's desk, or the way the walls are dingy and yellowed by smoke.

- Next focus on antonyms. Choose one adjective to revise them (for example, 'untidy' is an antonym for 'tidy', 'neat' or 'orderly'). Ask children to suggest antonyms for the other adjectives, again listing suggestions on the board. Reflect what kind of room their suggestions would describe (somewhere light, bright, airy, clean, tidy).

> **Differentiation**
> **Support:** Allow children to use a thesaurus or dictionary to help them find synonyms/antonyms.
>
> ---
>
> **Extension:** Children can draft a paragraph using antonyms to describe a pleasant, clean study that might be used by Professor Glastonberry.

2. List it

> **Objective**
> To use punctuation consistently for lists including colons and semicolons or bullets.
>
> **What you need**
> Copies of *Journey to the River Sea*, photocopiable page 22 'List it'.

What to do

- Arrange the children in pairs and tell them to skim and scan the description of the visit to Manaus (Chapter 4) for the many different things Maia sees. Bring the class back together and ask the children to suggest attractions they would include in a tourist brochure or website for visitors to Manaus. Note a few key ideas on the board.

- Referring back to the text, focus on the way the author sets out lists of things Maia sees, for example, the list beginning 'Everywhere were busy people' or the description of the crows. Highlight the use of the colon to introduce the list, and commas to separate words or phrases.

- List the attractions on the board, using the same punctuation. Demonstrate how they could also be written as lists using bullets or semicolons.

- Hand out photocopiable page 22 'List it' and tell the children to work in their pairs to fill them in. They can use colons and bullet points or semicolons.

> **Differentiation**
> **Support:** Work through one of the sections on the photocopiable page together to establish familiarity with the punctuation.
>
> ---
>
> **Extension:** Challenge children to devise and compile more lists using content from the novel.

3. It's a possibility

> ### Objective
> To use and understand modal verbs.
>
> ### What you need
> Copies of *Journey to the River Sea*.

What to do

- Re-read Extract 1, describing Maia's attempt to get to Manaus. Ask: *What could have happened to Maia?* Write the question and highlight the modal verb 'could'. Explain that it suggests something that was possible, but did not happen. Tell them that we use modal verbs to indicate things that are possible, and even to suggest how likely they are to happen. List on the board: 'can', 'could', 'may', 'might', 'shall', 'should', 'will', 'would', 'must'.

- Write on the board: 'Finn _____ go back to England.' Ask pairs to take turns saying the same sentence aloud, using different modal verbs: 'Finn can', 'Finn could', 'Finn may' and so on. They should then write down their answers. In each case, they should decide what the verb suggests: how likely is it that he will go? Which make it sound most likely that he will go back, and which least likely? (For example, 'Finn *will* go back to England' or 'Finn *must* go back' make it sound certain; 'Finn *should* go back to England', makes it sound as if people expect him to, but he may not.)

- When pairs have experimented with different modals, encourage them to share ideas, and attempt to rank them according to which verbs make it sound most likely, and which least.

> ### Differentiation
> **Support:** Write sentences about Finn using one or two modal verbs on the board and discuss what they imply before pairs begin.
>
> ---
>
> **Extension:** Challenge pairs to use modal verbs in sentences about other characters from the novel.

4. Pronoun power

> ### Objective
> To use relative clauses; to use commas to clarify meaning.
>
> ### What you need
> Copies of *Journey to the River Sea*, photocopiable page 23 'Pronoun power'.

What to do

- Re-read the beginning of Chapter 9, as far as 'drive him back to his old home'. Ask volunteers to think up a factual statement about Bernard, for example, 'Bernard Taverner was an explorer.'

- As a class, think how the statement could be extended using a relative pronoun ('who', 'which', 'when' and so on), for example 'Bernard Taverner was an explorer who ran away from Westwood.'

- Now challenge the children to use another pronoun to extend the sentence further. Write the sentences on the board, asking the children where to insert commas to help convey meaning and sense. For example, 'Bernard Taverner was an explorer who ran away from Westwood, which was his family home.'

- Hand out photocopiable page 23 'Pronoun power' and ask the children to work in pairs to fill it in. Remind them to use commas to show where there should be a pause in long sentences.

> ### Differentiation
> **Support:** Provide relevant facts to help the children extend the sentences on the photocopiable page, or work through the page as a shared activity, writing suggestions on the board.
>
> ---
>
> **Extension:** Children can work in pairs, writing more short factual statements about characters or topics in the novel and challenging their writing partner to use relative pronouns to extend them.

5. Verbs and voices

Objective
To use passive verbs to affect the presentation of information in a sentence.

What you need
Copies of *Journey to the River Sea*.

What to do
- Write these two sentences on the board: 'The crows took Clovis back to England. Clovis was taken back to England by the crows.' Underline the active and passive verbs. Ask the children how the verb affects the emphasis of the sentence (the active verb puts the focus on the crows, the passive on Clovis).

- Ask them to suggest a sentence to follow on, for example: 'The crows took Clovis back to England. They thought he was Taverner's son.' or 'Clovis was taken back to England by the crows. He pretended to be Taverner's son.'

- Write: 'Miss Minton threw the corset into the river.' Ask a volunteer to change the verb to the passive, dictating the new sentence for you to write on the board: 'The corset was thrown by Miss Minton into the river.' Can they suggest a follow-on sentence for each sentence following the same patternas above?

- List some items from the book on the board, for example:
  - The *Arabella*
  - The pocket watch
  - The glass eyeballs
- Challenge children to work in pairs to write a pair of sentences about each, following the same pattern using active and passive verbs.

Differentiation
Support: As a class, work through one or two sentences together, writing them on the board to make children familiar with the sentence pattern.

Extension: Challenge pairs to draft further pairs of sentences about topics from the novel using active and passive verbs, writing follow-on sentences for each.

6. Sounds the same

Objective
To distinguish between homophones and other words that are often confused.

What you need
Copies of *Journey to the River Sea*, photocopiable page 24 'Sounds the same'.

What to do
- Write the title of the book on the board and underline the word 'sea'. Ask the children if they can think of another word that sounds the same but has a different meaning ('see'). Challenge them to use each word in short sentences about the novel, for example, 'Maia travels by sea to Brazil.' 'Maia can see the Indian huts from her bedroom window.'

- Brainstorm some more examples of homophones on the board ('wood'/'would'; 'sort'/'sought'; 'air'/'heir'; 'team'/'teem' and so on). Ask volunteers to use one word and its homophone in sentences about someone or something in the novel to bring out its meaning, for example, 'The crows sought Bernard Taverner's son. Mr Carter liked to sort his eyeball collection.'

- Arrange the children in pairs and ask them to write some more sentences about topics in the novel using the homophones you have listed.

- Hand out photocopiable page 24 'Same sound, different meaning' and ask the children to choose a word from the box to fill the gap in each *a* sentence. They should write the correct homophone to fill the gap in each *b* sentence.

- Bring the class back together to review their sentences.

Differentiation
Support: Provide one answer for each pair of sentences on the photocopiable sheet and challenge children to find its homophone.

Extension: Challenge pairs of children to construct more sentences about characters or topics from the novel using homophones.

List it

- Make lists of the following topics. Use bullet points, colons or semicolons as needed.
- Draw an item from each list.

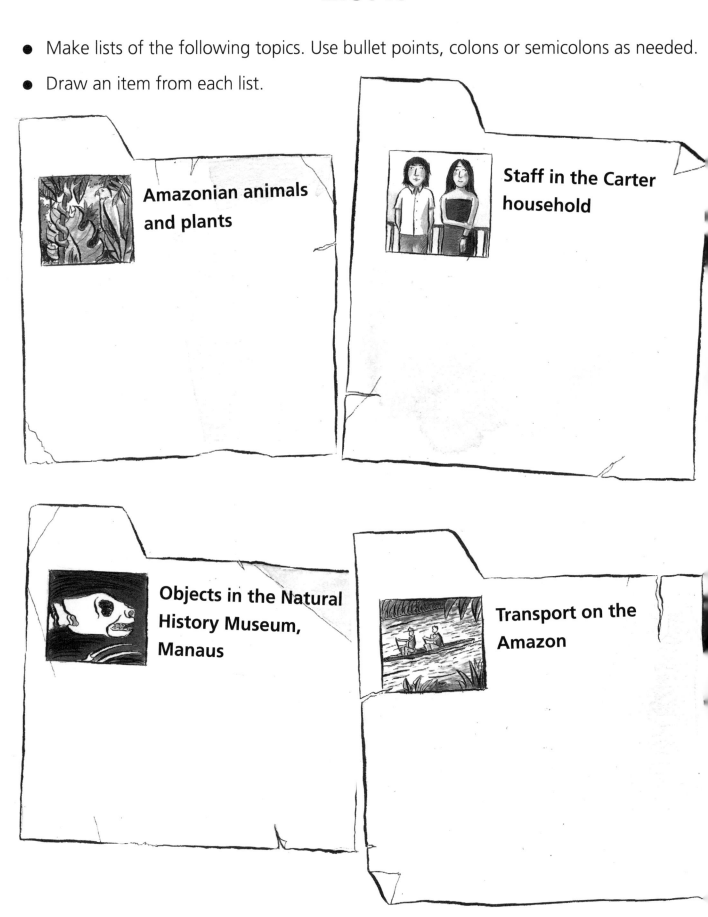

Amazonian animals and plants

Staff in the Carter household

Objects in the Natural History Museum, Manaus

Transport on the Amazon

Pronoun power

- Rewrite the following sentences, extending them by using relative pronouns ('who', 'when', 'which', 'where', 'that', 'whose'). Remember to use commas to divide clauses.

1. Maia was sent to live with the Carters.

_____

_____

2. Mr Murray had found Maia's relatives.

_____

_____

3. Clovis belonged to the Pilgrim Players.

_____

_____

4. The Carters lived in a bungalow.

_____

_____

5. Madame Duchamp ran a dance school.

_____

_____

6. The Goodleys adopted Clovis.

_____

_____

7. Colonel da Silva loved the theatre.

_____

_____

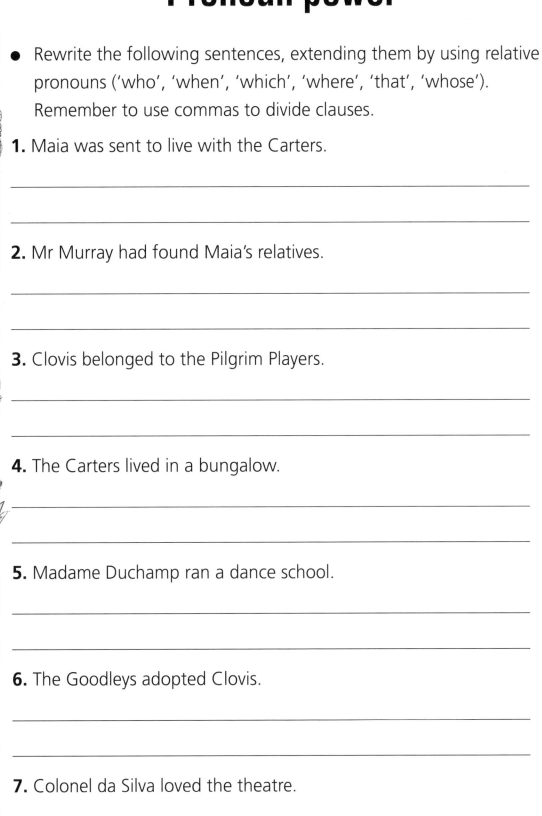

Sounds the same

● For each sentence **a** choose a word from the box below, then think of its homophone to fill the gap in each sentence **b**.

key   allowed   week   root   would   seller

1. a. Maia stumbled over the _____ of a tree.

   b. Finn followed the same _____ he had taken with Maia.

2. a. Maia had to steal the _____ to the Museum.

   b. The boat sailed from the _____ in Manaus.

3. a. The market _____ wore a brilliantly coloured bandanna.

   b. Clovis had to hide in the _____.

4. a. Maia was not _____ out on her own.

   b. Mrs Carter read the newspaper entry _____.

5. a. Finn thought the pocket watch _____ convince his grandfather.

   b. On the far side of the lake at Westwood, was a bluebell _____.

6. a. Maia's first _____ at the Carter's bungalow felt like being in prison.

   b. Mr Low was feeling _____ with a fever.

PLOT, CHARACTER & SETTING ▶

1. Storyboard

Objective
To identify main ideas drawn from more than one paragraph and to summarise these.

What you need
Copies of *Journey to the River Sea*, drawing materials.

Cross-curricular link
Art and design

What to do
- Read the passage in Chapter 13 from 'By the time they got to the museum...' to 'Then he followed the crows out of the museum.' Ask the children to summarise what happens and why Maia is at first so anxious, and then so surprised.

- Tell the children to imagine they are planning to film this scene for a movie. Explain that film-makers often make storyboards before filming: a sequence of pictures showing how the action develops.

- Arrange the children in pairs and let them re-read the episode. Encourage them to decide which scenes they are going to illustrate for their storyboard.

- In their pairs, ask the children to list six scenes, then write brief notes on what each scene should show. They should include notes on characters, action and setting.

- Let the children each draw out the storyboards they have briefed.

Differentiation
Support: Provide extra adult support in choosing the storyboard scenes. Accept fewer scenes

Extension: Let the children choose another episode in the novel to storyboard in notes and pictures.

2. The amazing Amazon

Objective
To distinguish between statements of fact and opinion.

What you need
Copies of *Journey to the River Sea*, photocopiable page 29 'The amazing Amazon'.

Cross-curricular link
Geography

What to do
- Tell the children that they are going to focus on the setting of the novel, and what we learn about the Amazon. Begin by asking them to recall any key facts, for example, which country is the book set in? What kind of animals are described?

- Tell the children to work in pairs to skim and scan the novel for facts about the Amazon. Encourage them to focus on chapters 1–5, 7, 14, 20–21 and 23. Remind them that they are not looking for opinions, but facts only. Discuss: *What kind of language might indicate an opinion rather than a fact?* (emotive/persuasive, judgemental) *What indicates a fact?* (neutral, non-judgemental.) Give examples of each: 'Everyone knows there are nasty, scary insects.' 'There are many varieties of insects, including butterflies and mosquitoes.'

- Hand out photocopiable page 29 'The amazing Amazon' and ask pairs to complete it.

- Bring the class back together and share ideas.

Differentiation
Support: Discuss where to find facts in the novel before children complete the sheet.

Extension: Challenge children to research in books or on the Internet to find more facts about the Amazon.

PLOT, CHARACTER & SETTING

3. Which country?

Objective
To ask relevant questions to extend their understanding and knowledge.

What you need
Copies of *Journey to the River Sea*.

What to do

- Focus on Clovis. Ask: *Can you recall how Maia first meets Clovis?* (sailing to Brazil on the *Cardinal*)

- Challenge the children to work in pairs and discuss how Clovis is important in the plot. Write questions on the board as prompts: *How did Clovis bring Maia and Finn together?* (Maia first meets Finn when she is attempting to get to Manaus to see Clovis' play.) *Why could the plot of the story not develop without him?* (He takes Finn's place and returns to Westwood, allowing Finn to stay on the Amazon.) Encourage them to skim and scan the novel for ideas. When they have finished, share ideas.

- Challenge pairs to repeat the exercise with another character such as Miss Minton or Professor Glastonberry. Ask: *In what ways are they important in the plot? What would not happen without them?* (For example, Professor Glastonberry provides the hiding place for Clovis in the cellar and helps Miss Minton find Finn and Maia.) Again, they should skim and scan the novel for ideas.

- Invite pairs to share ideas with the class, eliciting contributions for as many characters as possible.

Differentiation
Support: Provide questions to help guide children: *How does Maia meet this character? Could the story plot happen without them – if not, why not?*

Extension: Pairs can repeat the exercise for all key characters and rate them with 1–5 stars based on their importance in the plot.

4. Three orphans

Objective
To give well-structured descriptions, explanations and narratives.

What you need
Copies of *Journey to the River Sea*.

What to do

- Remind the children that Maia, Finn and Clovis all have one thing in common – they are orphans. Suggest that often in children's stories, the author makes the main character an orphan (invite suggestions of familiar characters from fiction, such as Harry Potter, Cinderella, Alex Rider). Can they suggest why? (Possibly because it allows the child a freer rein for adventures.)

- Arrange the class into groups of three. Each child should focus on one of the three orphans and make notes on:

  - Why they are orphans and what brings them to the Amazon.

  - How their character meets the other two characters.

  - How they contribute to the main plot line.

  - How the story ends for their character.

- When they have finished, the children should share ideas by discussing them in their groups. Then bring the class together and ask for volunteers from each group to share their findings, making brief notes on the board for each character to consolidate ideas. Encourage feedback and cross-checking of facts.

Differentiation
Support: Let children work in small groups focusing on one orphan, making sure the class as a whole covers all three characters.

Extension: Challenge children to list things that happen to their character that drive the plot. For example, Clovis meets Maia on the *Cardinal* and invites her to his play.

5. It's character building!

Objective

To draw inferences, such as describing characters' feelings, thoughts and motives from their actions; to describe characters.

What you need

Copies of *Journey to the River Sea*.

Cross-curricular link

PSHE

What to do

- As a class, find adjectives that describe characters and write them on the whiteboard ('kind', 'cruel', 'brave', 'cowardly', 'sensible', 'clever', 'dull', etc).

- Divide the class into small groups and ask each group to nominate a note-taker. Tell each group to choose a character from the story and decide on three adjectives that best describe them. They should use the list or think up their own, and support each choice by citing evidence from the story. (Maia is brave because she ventures out into the jungle on her own; she is kind because she wants to help Clovis get back to England.)

- Review their findings and encourage the class to challenge or support their statements.

- Briefly discuss devices the author uses to create our understanding of characters, writing headings on the board: 'physical description' (facial features, hair colour, clothes); 'habits' (for example, the twins echoing each other's movements); 'behaviour' (for example, the twins' nastiness towards Maia) and 'actions' (their betrayal of Finn for the reward money).

- Let children work in their groups to discuss and make notes on their character using these headings.

Differentiation

Support: Choose a character from the book and write one or two key facts under the headings 'physical description', 'behaviour', 'habits' and 'actions' on the board before they begin work.

Extension: Groups can repeat the exercise for another character or characters.

6. Predictions

Objective

To predict what might happen from details stated and implied.

What you need

Copies of *Journey to the River Sea*, photocopiable page 30 'Predictions'.

What to do

- Tell the children they are going to focus on 'plot hooks': devices the author uses to make us want to read on in the novel. Suggest that one way is raising questions we want answered; another by providing clues that encourage us to predict what might happen.

- Ask: *How did Maia feel when she was told she was being sent to live with distant relatives on the Amazon? Excited? A bit scared? What is the main hook that makes us want to read on?* (to find out what happens on her adventure)

- Arrange children into small groups and allocate each a key character or characters: Maia, Finn, Miss Minton, the Carters, the crows. Ask them to discuss questions the author raises about their character. For example: *Who is the mystery boy sought by the crows? What has happened in Miss Minton's past and how is she connected to the Amazon?*

- When they have identified two or three plot hooks, share ideas. Encourage them to think how the author encourages us to piece together facts to predict what might happen in the plot.

- Hand out photocopiable page 30 'Predictions' and ask children to work individually or in pairs to complete it.

Differentiation

Support: Provide a list of predictions for them to choose from.

Extension: Challenge pairs to identify more clues from the plot to extend the photocopiable page.

PLOT, CHARACTER & SETTING

7. Green hell or heaven?

Objective
To give well-structured descriptions, for different purposes; to draw inferences such as inferring characters' thoughts.

What you need
Copies of *Journey to the River Sea*, photocopiable page 29 'The amazing Amazon' (or children's completed copies from Lesson 2 in this section).

Cross-curricular link
PSHE

What to do

- Remind the children of the quote Maia reads in the school library before she leaves England, that the Amazon can be either a 'Green Hell…or a heaven'. Re-read the paragraph from Chapter 1 together. Ask them to suggest characters in the novel who represent these two opposing views (Finn and Maia see it as heaven; the Carters and the crows see it as hell).

- Provide photocopiable page 29 for reference, and ask the children to think how different characters view each aspect of life on the Amazon. For example, the Carters see the Indian people as ignorant savages; Finn and Maia see them as a kind, wise and skilled people.

- Children should work in their pairs, one voicing 'hell', the other 'heaven'. They should take turns to think up and say aloud a statement expressing how their character feels or thinks about each topic. For example, one of the twins would say 'The forest is a dangerous and horrible place', whereas Maia might say, 'The forest is a magical and beautiful place'.

Differentiation
Support: Limit the task to three or four topics from the photocopiable page.

Extension: Let children discuss in their pairs how all the key characters see the different aspects of life and how the author conveys their attitudes through actions as well as speech.

8. Good point, bad point

Objective
To give well-structured explanations.

What you need
Copies of *Journey to the River Sea*, photocopiable page 31 'Good point, bad point'.

Cross-curricular link
PSHE

What to do

- Tell the children they are going to think about the main characters in the story, and decide what their good points and bad points are. Before they begin, invite volunteers to voice one good point and one bad point about themselves. For example, they may be kind (good point) but untidy (bad point).

- Brainstorm good and bad character traits: for example (good) kind, brave, strong; (bad) unkind, cowardly, weak. Note the best suggestions under the headings 'Good points' and 'Bad points' on the board.

- Hand out photocopiable page 31 'Good point, bad point' and let children work in pairs to fill it in.

- When they have finished, invite volunteers from pairs to read out their statements, and encourage feedback and criticism. Ask: *How hard was it to find good points about the nasty characters? Are points listed as 'bad' always negative?* (For example, Clovis is nervous, but do we like him any less for it, or does it make him more likeable and funny?) *Are points listed as 'good' always positive?* (For example, the twins are determined but only to get their own way and benefit themselves.)

Differentiation
Support: Limit the task to writing one or two points for each character.

Extension: Pairs should extend their statements by providing evidence from the story.

The amazing Amazon

● Write down facts that we learn about the Amazon from the novel.

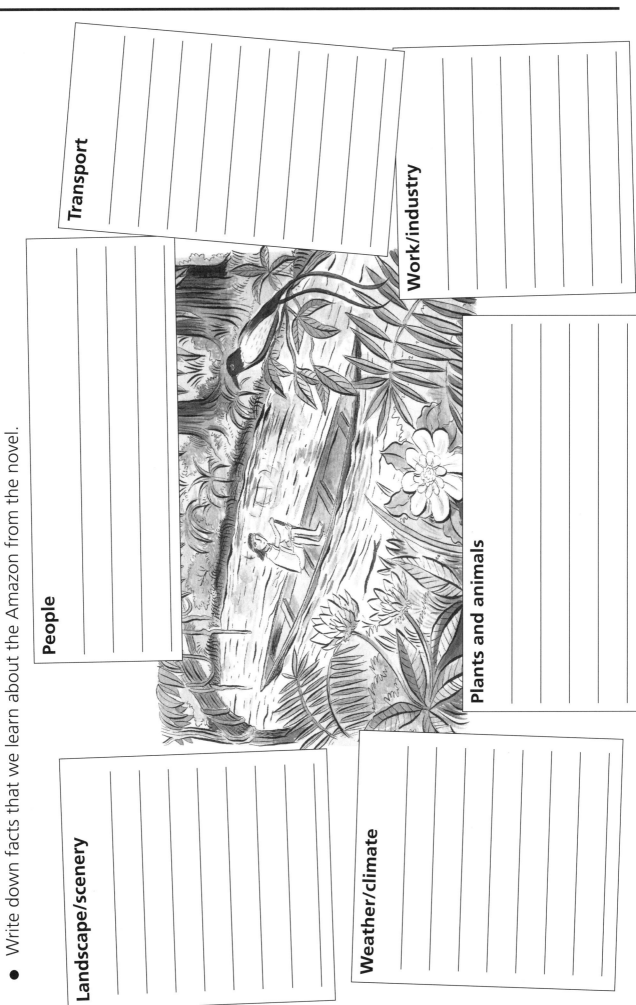

Transport

People

Work/industry

Plants and animals

Landscape/scenery

Weather/climate

Predictions

- Draw a line to match a clue to each fact and then write a prediction of what will happen in the plot.

Fact	Clue	Prediction
• Westwood needs a new cook.	• Miss Minton has a bad migraine on the night of Clovis' theatre play.	
• Finn is wanted back in England but does not want to go.	• Miss Minton is fed up with working for the Carters.	
• Finn feels something holding him back on his journey to the Xanti.	• Clovis is homesick for England.	
• Maia is desperate to keep her promise to see Clovis at the theatre in Manaus.	• Clovis' foster mother is a very good cook.	
• The Keminskys' governess is leaving.	• Maia wants to go with Finn on his journey to the Xanti.	

Good point, bad point

● Write down some good points and some bad points about each character. You can choose from the list below or think of your own.

brave	strong	impulsive	foolhardy
cowardly	nervous	kind	bad tempered
impatient	patient	determined	trustworthy

	Good points	Bad points
Maia		
Finn		
Clovis		

● Write a statement about each character, using ideas from the table above. Give evidence from the text if you can.

1. _____

_____

2. _____

_____

3. _____

_____

● Choose a character in the story who has mostly bad points. Try to write down least one good point he or she has.

Character: _____

Bad points	Good points

TALK ABOUT IT ▶

1. Fairytale villains

> ### Objective
> To participate in role play, improvisations and debates.
>
> ### What you need
> Copies of *Journey to the River Sea*.

What to do

- Remind the children that Maia sometimes feels like Cinderella when she is living at the Carters'. Ask: *What does this make the twins?* (the ugly sisters) Brainstorm how Gwendolyn and Beatrice are like the ugly sisters (their ridiculous clothes, their nastiness, greed, jealousy, the way they act in unison and so on).

- Arrange the class into groups of four. Tell them they are going to improvise a scene in which Maia tries to persuade Mrs Carter and the twins to let her go to see Clovis' play. They should first re-read Chapter 4 from 'They were to meet the Carters at the theatre…' as far as 'And they followed their mother to the waiting cab'. Children should then decide their roles and consider what their character is thinking/feeling before they begin the improvisation. For example, Maia is upset and worried because she does not want to let Clovis down.

- Observe as groups improvise the scene and invite one or two of the most successful groups to perform it for the class. Encourage constructive feedback and comments.

- Finish by discussing why the children think the twins behave as they do. (Are they spoiled? If so, how? What are the Carters like as parents and role models?)

> ### Differentiation
> **Support:** Before groups begin, discuss together the motivations of each character.

2. Nature study

> ### Objective
> To maintain attention and participate actively in collaborative conversations.
>
> ### What you need
> Copies of *Journey to the River Sea*.
>
> ### Cross-curricular link
> Science

What to do

- Remind the children that the author's husband was a keen naturalist. Which characters in the book share his passion? (Bernard Taverner and Finn, Professor Glastonberry, Miss Minton, Maia)

- Re-read together the first half of Chapter 9. Ask: *What important facts do we learn about Bernard?* (He was nervous and timid but loved animals and nature.)

- Brainstorm a few key words for the qualities a good naturalist needs: a curious or enquiring mind, love of the natural world/science, patience.

- Arrange the class into small groups. Ask them to think how the five characters named above demonstrate the qualities a good naturalist needs. For example: Professor Glastonberry is a good naturalist because he has the patience to reassemble the sloth skeleton. They should skim and scan the novel for evidence.

- Allow them time to discuss, then invite volunteers from each group to make statements about different characters, supporting them with evidence.

> ### Differentiation
> **Support:** Let groups focus on Bernard Taverner.
>
> ---
>
> **Extension:** Let groups discuss how the work of a naturalist today may be different from how it was in 1910 when the novel is set.

3. Journeys

Objective
To use spoken language to develop understanding; to participate in discussions.

What you need
Copies of *Journey to the River Sea.*

Cross-curricular links
PSHE, geography

What to do
- Focus attention on the word 'Journey' in the title of the book and ask the children to summarise the main journey in the narrative (Maia's journey from England to the Amazon). Suggest that as well as the physical journey, a journey can often be a 'voyage of discovery'. People often see journeys as a way to explore places and also to discover things about themselves.

- Encourage volunteers to talk about journeys they have made, and what they learned from them or about themselves. It might be somewhere they especially liked or disliked, or that they discovered something they could do they had never tried before. Encourage discussion of how journeys can open our minds.

- Arrange the class into pairs and challenge them to think of three things that Maia learns about the Amazon, and three things she learns about herself. Bring the class back together and note the best ideas on the board. (For example, Maia learns about the Xanti, the waterways and Manaus; and she learns that she is brave; keen for adventure and loves the Amazon.)

Differentiation
Support: Limit the pair task to what Maia learns about the Amazon, then discuss as a class what she discovers about herself.

Extension: Let pairs repeat the exercise for other characters (for example, Clovis or Miss Minton).

4. Consequences

Objective
To give well-structured explanations for different purposes.

What you need
Copies of *Journey to the River Sea*, photocopiable page 35 'Consequences', scissors, glue and paper.

What to do
- Arrange the class in pairs and hand out copies of photocopiable page 35 'Consequences'. Explain that they should work through the sheet, discussing how each event drives the plot. Discuss the first event together, to get them started: When Miss Minton's corset is found floating, it leads to the search party that finds Maia and Finn living amongst the Xanti, meaning they must return to England.

- When they have finished, they should cut out the boxes and paste them on the paper in the order they appear *in the narrative*. Point out that this may not be the same as their chronological order, the order in which they happened in time.

- Review their work as a class. Encourage children to think how the author sometimes shifts the narrative back in time, to explain events: for example, the horse riding accident happened sometime in the past, but it does not appear in the narrative until Chapter 9.

Differentiation
Support: Provide chapter references for events in the novel to help children arrange events in the right order: Box 5: Chapter 1; Box 3: Chapter 6; Box 4: Chapter 9; Box 2: Chapter 9; Box 6: Chapter 18; Box 1: Chapter 23.

Extension: Pairs can think of other events that drive the plot, discussing them together before writing or drawing them and arranging them in the right order.

5. True or view?

> **Objective**
> To distinguish between statements of fact and opinion.
>
> **What you need**
> Copies of *Journey to the River Sea*, photocopiable page 36 'True or view?'
>
> **Cross-curricular links**
> Geography, PSHE, citizenship

What to do

- Tell the children they are going to focus on the Indian peoples who are the native or indigenous peoples of the Amazon. With appropriate sensitivity to different ethnicities and cultures, begin by discussing the Carters' view of the Indians (they are stupid, ignorant, dirty – as expressed in Chapter 3) and Maia and Finn's view of them (they are skilled, clever, kind). Remind children that the girls at Maia's school voiced opinions about the Indians that turned out to be false (in Chapter 1 Anna warns they might shoot her with poisoned arrows). Emphasise that these are subjective opinions about the Indians.

- Ask the children to volunteer any true facts we learn about the Indians from the novel, and write them on the board (for example, they belong to tribes such as the Tapuri and Xanti).

- Hand out photocopiable page 36 'True or view?' and ask pairs to briefly discuss it. Then have a class discussion about each statement before deciding whether it is a true fact or a view.

- Consider how the novel teaches us some true facts about the indigenous Indians, but also shows us how they are viewed by different characters. Ask: *What do you think the author thought of the Indians and why?*

> **Differentiation**
> **Extension:** Challenge children to compile a factfile about the Indians.

6. White lies

> **Objective**
> To use spoken language to develop understanding through speculating, hypothesising, imagining and exploring ideas.
>
> **What you need**
> Copies of *Journey to the River Sea*, photocopiable page 37 'Deceptions'.
>
> **Cross-curricular link**
> PSHE

What to do

- Start by suggesting to the children that the happy ending that comes about for all the good or likeable characters in the novel is based on a lie or deception. Challenge them to explain why (Clovis pretends to be Sir Aubrey's grandson, deceiving him about the truth). Ask: *Do you think the deception is justified? Is it a 'white lie' and, if so, how and why?* (Sir Aubrey might die if he were told the truth and then Finn would have to return; he wants to stay on the Amazon, while Clovis is happy at Westwood. The white lie keeps everyone happy.)

- Discuss the concept of a white lie, and ask the children if they can suggest any examples in their own lives, and why a white lie might sometimes be justified. (Perhaps if the truth would upset someone or make them unhappy?) Suggest that the motivation is important: is it for the well-being of others or just for self-interest?

- Hand out photocopiable page 37 'Deceptions' and ask children to work in pairs to complete it.

> **Differentiation**
> **Support:** Read through the statements together before pairs begin, discussing their context in the novel.
>
> ---
>
> **Extension:** Let pairs discuss other novels where deceptions lead to a happy ending and how they are justified (for example, Roald Dahl's *Danny Champion of the World*).

Consequences

- Explain the consequence of each event and how it drives the plot forward.
- Then cut and paste the events in the order they appear in the narrative.

1. A corset found floating

2. A letter from a magazine editor

3. A boy's voice breaking

4. A horse riding accident

5. A train crash

6. A house fire

True or view?

● Tick the box to show whether the statement is a true fact or a view on the Indians in the story.

The Indians	True	View
They mix Portuguese in with their own language		
They are hunter-gatherers		
The women weave hammocks and basket		
They want to cheat you		
They are skilled hunters of deer, pigs and bush turkeys		
They keep dogs, monkeys and spiders and tame birds as pets		
They sometimes paint their bodies		
They shoot people with poisoned arrows		
Their food is dirty and full of germs		

Deceptions

● Tick the box to say whether you think the action is right or wrong then give your reasons.

Action	Right?	Wrong?	Explain why
Miss Minton pretends Maia is too slow to keep up with the twins in lessons.			_____ _____ _____ _____
Mr Carter does not forward Miss Minton's letter about Clovis to Mr Murray.			_____ _____ _____ _____
Mr Carter promises to protect the 'Tapherini' longhouse then pulls it down.			_____ _____ _____ _____
Miss Minton pretends to recognise Clovis as Finn Taverner as he comes out of the cellar.			_____ _____ _____ _____
Clovis tells Sir Aubrey he really is his grandson.			_____ _____ _____ _____

GET WRITING ▶

1. Mrs Carter's house rules

Objective
To identify the audience for and purpose of the writing, selecting the appropriate form.

What you need
Copies of *Journey to the River Sea*, photocopiable page 41 'Mrs Carter's house rules'.

What to do

- Re-read Chapter 3 together. Tell the children they are going to focus on life at the Carters' bungalow, and the kind of home the Carters have created. How would they describe it? (dull, clinical, prison-like?)

- Explain that they are going to draft some house rules that Mrs Carter might use, and invite suggestions. Discuss different ways to express rules or instructions: often beginning with 'Do' or 'Don't'; using imperative verbs such as 'Clean' or 'Use'; using modal verbs such as 'shall' or 'must'. Give some examples: The governess must have supper in her room. Only British food shall be served at the table. Use fly spray daily.

- Arrange the children into small groups and hand out photocopiable page 41 'Mrs Carter's house rules' for them to complete. Challenge children to work in their groups to list the rules, including daily tasks (such as using the flit gun and checking the ceilings for spiders).

- Share ideas and encourage feedback.

Differentiation
Support: Model rules under one heading on the board before groups begin.

Extension: Encourage groups to compare and contrast different homes in the novel: the Carters', Finn's, the Indians', the Keminskys', Lady Parsons' and say which they would like to live in most and why.

2. A letter home

Objective
To note and develop initial ideas, drawing on reading where necessary.

What you need
Copies of *Journey to the River Sea*.

What to do

- Remind the children that Maia's friends at school in England make her promise to write 'lots and lots of letters'. Tell them they are going to compose a letter that Maia might write and send to her friends at school after a few weeks in the Amazon.

- Before they begin, encourage them to think about the tone of Maia's letter. Ask: *In these first few weeks, how is she feeling about her new life?* (For example, she is dismayed at the twins and living with the Carters, but also enjoying observing the Indians and going to dance classes.)

- Arrange the children in pairs. Tell them to skim and scan the first four chapters for content, deciding what Maia might want to include in a letter to tell her friends about her new life.

- They should work together to make brief notes of the main topics to cover in the letter: the Carters and the twins; the surroundings and Indians, and so on. When they have made a list of topics, they should then work individually to draft a letter, making sure they set it out, address and sign it using the appropriate letter form.

- Invite volunteers to read their letters aloud, encouraging feedback and constructive criticism.

Differentiation
Support: Let children limit their letter to two or three topics.

Extension: Let pairs draft another letter to Maia's school friends based on events later in the novel.

3. Visit Manaus

Objective

To select the appropriate form using other similar writing as models for their own.

What you need

Copies of *Journey to the River Sea*, online examples of tourism materials from early 1900s, photocopiable page 42 'Visit Manaus'.

Cross-curricular link

Geography

What to do

- Tell the children they are going to focus on the descriptions of Manaus in the novel, and use them to compose a guide for tourists visiting the city in the early 1900s. Begin by reading together the first paragraph of the author's note describing how hearing about Manaus triggered the idea for the novel. Then re-read the key sections in Chapter 4 describing Manaus.

- If possible, view tourism materials from the early 1900s online, and discuss how the persuasive tone and the content is designed to encourage tourists to visit.

- Arrange children in pairs and ask them to skim and scan the text for key facts about Manaus.

- Hand out photocopiable page 42 'Visit Manaus' and tell pairs to use their notes to help them complete the guide. Briefly discuss ideas for each section before they begin (for example, 'Things to see' might include the theatre and museum; 'Things to do' might include a horse-drawn cab ride).

Differentiation

Support: When children have made notes, discuss together what they might include in a guide before they begin work on the photocopiable sheet.

Extension: Challenge children to use another copy of the photocopiable sheet to compile a guide to Manaus today, using their own research.

4. Looking for Bernard

Objective

To identify the audience for and purpose of the writing, selecting the appropriate form.

What you need

Copies of *Journey to the River Sea*.

What to do

- Re-read together the part of Chapter 9 focusing on Sir Aubrey's search for his son Bernard, and then his grandson (from 'And so the years passed' to 'And two months later, the crows arrived in Manaus').

- As a class, draft the advertisement that Sir Aubrey might place in *The Times* and other newspapers. Explain that this kind of advertisement sometimes appears when solicitors are seeking relatives who may be heirs to an estate. Discuss the wording, considering what it should and should not include: for example, Sir Aubrey will not want to give too much away but he will want to persuade Bernard to respond. Invite or suggest ideas for the heading and write the advertisement on the board, encouraging constructive feedback.

- Remind the children that when Sir Aubrey discovers Bernard has died, he writes a letter to Bernard's son, sending copies to Bernard's bank manager and a Manaus post box. Arrange them in pairs and tell them to try drafting this letter. Again, they should consider what kind of information Sir Aubrey would include, and the persuasive tone he would use to encourage Bernard's son to come home to Westwood.

- Invite volunteers to read out their letters, again encouraging constructive criticism.

Differentiation

Support: Discuss the content of the letter, summarising events at Westwood before pairs begin.

Extension: Let pairs discuss how Finn might feel reading the letter, then draft the letter he might write if he had replied.

5. Painting with words

Objective

To discuss and evaluate how authors use language, including figurative language, considering the impact on the reader.

What you need

Copies of *Journey to the River Sea*, photocopiable page 43 'Painting with words'.

What to do

- Tell the children that they are going to focus on the author's language and, in particular, her use of figurative language, including similes and metaphors. Before they begin, briefly revise both by writing on the board:

  - Behind her, the jungle closed like a green curtain (simile).

  - The green curtain of the jungle closed behind her (metaphor).

- Encourage the children to consider how comparing the undergrowth of the jungle to a green curtain helps the reader visualise it, and how much more effective the simile and metaphor are than saying simply 'the jungle was very dense and green'.

- Hand out photocopiable page 43 'Painting with words' and let children work in pairs to complete it. When they have finished, bring the class back together to review their work. Which similes and metaphors do the children find most effective and why?

- Challenge pairs to write a sentence using a simile or a metaphor to describe three things Maia sees in the Amazon jungle.

Differentiation

Extension: Challenge pairs to write more sentences containing similes or metaphors describing characters or places in the novel.

6. Mr Trapwood's diary

Objective

To draw inferences, such as inferring characters' feelings, thoughts and motives from their actions.

What you need

Copies of *Journey to the River Sea*.

Cross-curricular link

PSHE

What to do

- Focus on the crows. Ask: *What do their characters contribute to the novel?* (They are hunting for Finn, so add tension to the plot; there is humour in their hapless attempts and the way the locals dupe them.)

- Explain that the children are going to draft a diary entry that Mr Trapwood might write on the day the crows decide to give up the search and return to England.

- Briefly review key features of diary writing (first person, past tense, may be informal writing; may include reflective/subjective emotions). Can the children think of any famous books that are written in diary form? (*The Diary of a Young Girl* by Anne Frank, *The Diary of a Killer Cat* by Anne Fine and *The Secret Diary of Adrian Mole Aged 13¾* by Sue Townsend, for example)

- Ask them to skim and scan the novel, making notes of key episodes in the crows' search. Encourage them to try to convey Mr Trapwood's feelings, and to make it funny if they can.

- Invite volunteers to read aloud their diary entries.

Differentiation

Support: Provide question prompts when they are writing their diary entries. Ask: What are the main events that happen? How do they make Mr Trapwood feel? How does Mr Trapwood feel about Brazil?

Extension: The children write another entry, for example from the point of view of one of the crows describing the day they go to search for Finn in the cellar.

Mrs Carter's house rules

● Write down Mrs Carter's house rules for the bungalow.

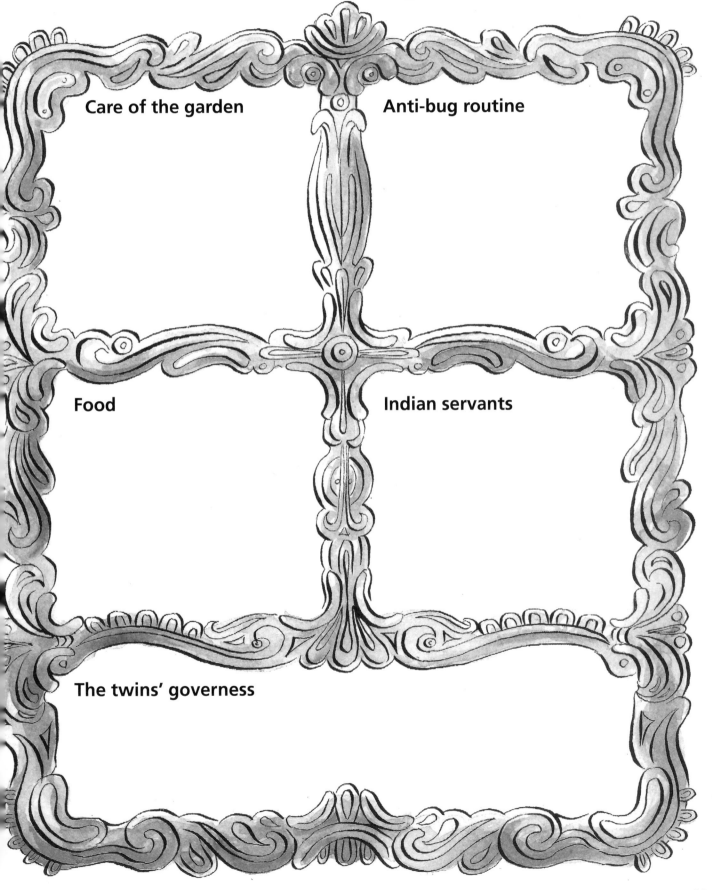

Care of the garden

Anti-bug routine

Food

Indian servants

The twins' governess

Visit Manaus

- Use your notes about Manaus to complete this tourist guide.

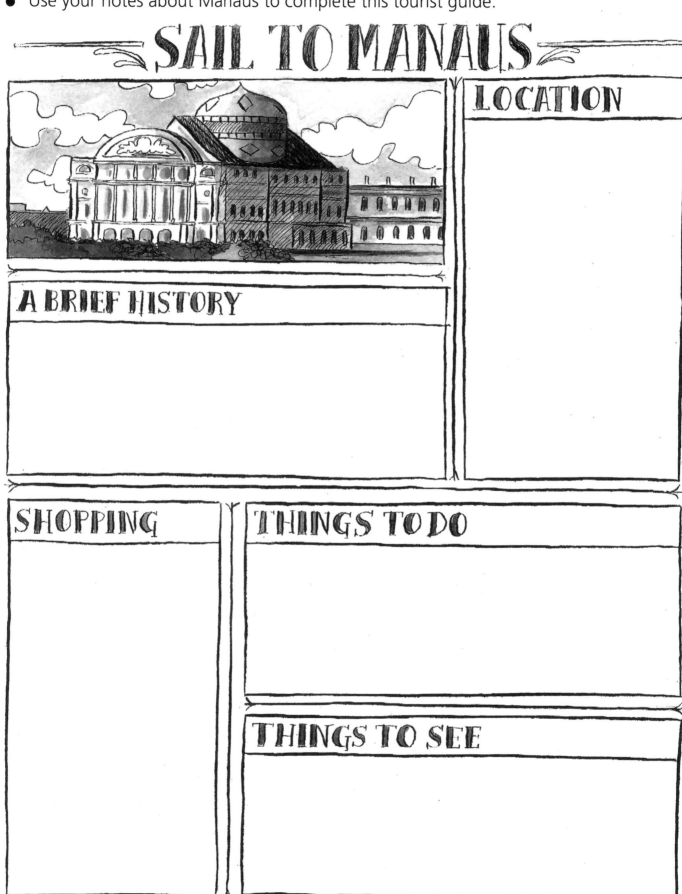

SAIL TO MANAUS

LOCATION

A BRIEF HISTORY

SHOPPING

THINGS TO DO

THINGS TO SEE

Painting with words

● Draw a line to match the subjects to the phrases that describe them. Then briefly explain the comparison.

Phrase: The crows

Phrase: A jewel in a shaft of sun

Phrase: You turn as yellow as a lemon

Phrase: A green curtain

Phrase: Hams in a butcher's shop

Subject: A scarlet orchid

_____

_____

_____

Subject: Mr Low and Mr Trapwood

_____

_____

_____

Subject: The twins' necks

_____

_____

Subject: The jungle

_____

_____

Subject: Yellow Fever

_____

_____

ASSESSMENT ▶

1. Chapter and title

Objective

To summarise the main ideas drawn from more than one paragraph.

What you need

Copies of *Journey to the River Sea*.

What to do

- Ask the children if they can summarise the main locations where the narrative takes place in the novel (Maia's school, the Amazon, Westwood, the Xanti territory).

- Can they suggest any other ways of separating out different threads from the narrative? (For example, Maia's life with the Carters, the crows' search for Finn, Clovis' wish to return to England.)

- Point out that the author has only used chapter numbers, not titles. Tell the children they are going to skim and scan the chapters and think up titles for some of them. The titles should give an idea of the content of the chapter without giving away too much of the plot.

- Brainstorm some ideas for the first chapter and write them on the board (for example, 'The adventure begins' or 'Leaving England').

- Arrange the children into small groups and assign each group up to four chapters. They should skim and scan the chapters to find a suitable title for each one. Allow them time to think up and list their ideas, then bring the class back together to share and review their titles.

Differentiation

Support: Let groups find titles for one or two chapters.

Extension: Challenge groups to think up possible titles for a sequel to the novel, given the way it ends. Have a class vote on the best idea.

2. Thinking about themes

Objective

To identify and discuss themes.

What you need

Copies of *Journey to the River Sea*.

What to do

- Begin by asking the children if they can identify what they think are the main themes of the novel. Brainstorm some ideas and note key words or phrases on the board (for example: 'learning from a journey', 'friendship', 'following your heart').

- Ask volunteers to state what they think is the main theme, supporting their statement with reasons. For example: I think the novel is about following your heart because Maia, Finn and Clovis all get to follow their hearts in the end; or, I think the novel is about friendship because Maia makes good friends.

- Prompt ideas with questions: *What theme might the Carters' attitude towards Brazil and the Indians represent?* (a criticism of colonials – people from a foreign power who occupy a country)

- Ask children to choose what they think is the most important theme of the novel, and write a short paragraph explaining why.

- Invite volunteers to read their paragraphs aloud, encouraging constructive feedback.

Differentiation

Support: Write a list of themes on the board and invite children to explain how they feature in the novel: 'learning from a journey', 'friendship', 'following your heart', 'changing your destiny', 'family and blood-ties'; 'colonialism /racism'.

Extension: Let children extend the writing work by describing all the main themes they can identify.

3. Plot picks

Objective

To summarise the main ideas drawn from more than one paragraph.

What you need

Copies of *Journey to the River Sea*, flash cards with names of key characters (Finn, Maia, Clovis, Miss Minton, Professor Glastonberry, the crows), stopwatch, photocopiable page 47 'Plot picks'.

What to do

- Tell the children they are going to try to summarise how key characters are important to the plot in as concise a way as possible. Explain that you will hold up flash cards with characters' names, and volunteers should then summarise in as few words and as short a time as possible, how they are important to the plot. They should follow the same sentence pattern saying: 'Professor Glastonberry is important to the plot because…'

- Model one example for them: 'Professor Glastonberry is important to the plot because he wants to help Finn and he lets Maia take the museum keys so Clovis can hide and be mistaken for Finn by the crows. He also helps Miss Minton to go after Maia and Finn in the Carters' boat.'

- Challenge each volunteer to summarise key points in 20 seconds, using the stopwatch.

- Tell the children they are now going to do the same exercise, focusing on objects that feature in the plot. Hand out photocopiable page 47 'Plot picks' and allow children time to complete it.

Differentiation

Support: Before children begin the written work, briefly discuss the context of each item on the photocopiable page.

Extension: Challenge children to extend the photocopiable page by sketching other items that feature in the plot, briefly explaining their significance.

4. Additions

Objective

To explain and discuss their understanding of what they have read; to provide reasoned justifications for their views.

What you need

Copies of *Journey to the River Sea*.

What to do

- Read aloud any reviews quoted in your edition of the novel and discuss the content with the children, reflecting on the qualities they highlight, and how far the children agree with them. Refer to the *Sunday Times* newspaper review from the back cover of the Macmillan edition of the novel ('The most perfect children's book… captivatingly told, funny and moving').

- Arrange the children in small groups and ask them to nominate a note taker who can take down ideas under headings. Ask them to discuss the content of the review, and what they think the reviewer means: for example, in what ways is the story 'captivatingly told'? In what ways is it 'funny' and how is it 'moving'? What do they think the reviewer means by calling it 'the most perfect children's book' and do they agree?

- Bring the class back together to review and discuss their findings.

- Challenge groups to draft another short review for the novel which could appear on the back cover and which would make readers want to read the book. Encourage them to try and identify different aspects of the novel, for example, the humour, the exotic setting, or the tightly woven plot. Invite volunteers to present their review to the class, and encourage feedback.

Differentiation

Support: Before groups begin, brainstorm ideas together on aspects they may want to include, making notes on the board.

Extension: Groups can prepare a short presentation for the class, explaining and supporting the ideas behind their reviews.

5. Amazon quiz

Objective

To explain and discuss their understanding of what they have read; to provide reasoned justifications for their views.

What you need

Copies of *Journey to the River Sea*.

What to do

- Tell the children they are going to compile quiz questions about the novel. Arrange them into small groups and allow them time to compile a quiz of six 'true and false' questions. They should skim and scan the novel for ideas for questions. They should appoint one note-taker to write down their questions and another to keep a list of correct answers.

- Model examples on the board:

  - The Carters' boat is called The Arabella: true or false? Answer: False

  - The fire boat is the Indians' name for the Carters' boat: true or false? Answer: True

- Groups can then challenge each other to answer their quiz questions, without referring back to the novel.

- Allow time for them to answer the questions. When they have finished, review scores and announce winning teams or groups.

- Encourage feedback, identifying which quiz questions were most challenging and why (where there might be confusion between the names of two boats that feature in the story, for example).

Differentiation

Support: Let children concentrate on questions based on one topic, such as characters in the novel, or questions about the setting.

Extension: Groups can write more than six true or false questions or they can attempt to devise a more challenging quiz about the novel, for example, a multiple-choice quiz or a quiz with a mixture of question types.

6. A classic adventure

Objective

To ask questions to improve their understanding; to use spoken language to develop understanding.

What you need

Copies of *Journey to the River Sea*.

What to do

- Using the tag 'classic adventure', which the novel has earned from critics, ask the children if they can suggest the key elements of an adventure story. These could include: hero/heroine who sets out on a journey or quest; an exotic or challenging setting; a fast, exciting pace with twists and turns in the plot; obstacles or nasty/villainous characters that stand in their way; resolution as the goal or journey's end is reached. Where possible, refer to other adventure stories that the children have read as a class, or with which they are familiar.

- List the key points on the board. Explain that they should use the list as headings, and make notes under each heading explaining how the novel fits into the genre. For example: 'Heroine': Maia; 'Journey': travels to the Amazon to start a new life; 'Exotic or challenging setting': the Amazon in Brazil.

- They should then use their notes to draft sentences under each heading, explaining how the novel fits into the genre of a 'classic adventure'.

- Bring the class back together to share findings, inviting volunteers to read their explanations aloud.

Differentiation

Support: Let children work in pairs and provide them with a list of the key elements for an adventure story, as discussed at the start of the lesson.

Extension: Encourage children to choose another adventure story and repeat the task, comparing and contrasting the two novels.

Plot picks

- Briefly explain how each of the following features in the plot.

1. A sloth skeleton 	**2.** A pocket watch 
3. An Edwardian corset 	**4.** A naval portrait 
5. A glass eyeball 	**6.** A handkerchief with the initial 'A' embroidered on it 

- Choose one item which you think is most important in driving the plot and explain why.

Notes